THE PRICE OF BEING ALIVE

may God always bless you, but never suffer you.

R. Landis Coffman

THE PRICE
OF BEING ALIVE

a fresh way to understand suffering

by R. Landis Coffman, Jr.

THE PRICE OF BEING ALIVE
A Fresh Way to Understand Suffering

Copyright © 2012 R. Landis Coffman, Jr. All rights reserved. Except for brief quotations in critical articles or reviews, no part of this book may be reproduced in any matter without prior permission from the author.

Scripture quotations marked (NIV) are taken from the Holy Bible, New International Version®, NIV®. Copyright © 1973, 1978, 1984, 2011 by Biblica, Inc.™ All rights reserved worldwide.

Scripture quotations marked (NRSV) are taken from the Revised Standard Version of the Bible, copyright 1952 [2nd edition, 1971] by the Division of Christian Education of the National Council of the Churches of Christ in the United States of America. Used by permission. All rights reserved.

Cover images: senior woman © Martina Ebel / iStockphoto.com; calico cat © Erik Zunec / iStock photo.com; boy © Jani Bryson / iStockphoto.com; solar nebula © Karl Dolenc / iStockphoto.com; young man © Ana Abejon / iStockphoto.com; foundry furnace © Aydın Mutlu / iStockphoto.com; preschool girl © Jarek Szymanski / iStockphoto.com; daisy © Amanda Rohde / iStockphoto.com; golden retriever © Kari Høglund / iStockphoto.com; penny © David Shultz / iStockphoto.com

Publishing consultant: Huff Publishing Associates, LLC
Cover and book design: Hillspring Books, Inc.

ISBN 978-0-615-58706-6

contents

Preface	9
1. Voices	11
2. Direction	15
3. The First Constant: God Is Love	19
4. The Second Constant: God Is Just	25
5. The Third Constant: God Is One	27
6. A New Answer, A New Theology	31
7. A New Answer Comes from Far Away	47
8. Satan	53
9. Suffering Is a Part of Life	63
10. God Can Work Through Suffering	73
11. Closing Thoughts	81
Epilogue	87
Acknowledgments	89
Biography	91

I dedicate this book to Charlotte Holzy and Susan Wright.

These two ladies experienced more intense suffering in their years than any person I knew in forty-four years of ministry. And at the end of their physical lives, they deeply loved the Lord their God. Peace.

preface

This book is for everyone, for the reality is that everyone suffers. Suffering has been a mystery ever since human life began. All religions have commented on this reality of life. Yet all of us continue to search for new ways to understand suffering. This book will throw some retardant on a fire that burns so hot that it damages human hearts and lives.

In this book I will use a Judeo-Christian structure on which to hang some basic tenets about how we might understand suffering. I will illustrate with stories and imagery to give a new view to an old enigma. No matter which religion you espouse, the practical material will give you a new way to think about suffering.

Come give this little book a good read. I believe that you will be challenged and awakened to a new perception of an old and encompassing problem of human existence.

CHAPTER ONE

VOICES

From early on in my ministry, I have heard all kinds of statements and questions about suffering. Some were observations. Some were teachings from the past. Some were wisdom from those who were suffering. Below is a long list of the statements and questions I have read and heard about suffering over the years. You could certainly add to the list.

- Why? Why me? Why us?
- What did I ever do to deserve this?
- Why is God doing this to me?
- Why has this happened to me?
- If I am a good person or a good Christian or a good _____, why should I suffer so much or suffer at all?
- Why does God allow suffering?
- It's not fair.
- Why do the innocent suffer?
- It's God's will!
- Suffering draws us to God.

12 The Price of Being Alive

- Through suffering God disciplines us.
- Through suffering God chastises us.
- We should see suffering as a gift from God to make us better people!
- God sends suffering to purify us and strengthen us.
- Your present suffering is proof that God loves you.
- God punishes like a parent does a child to help us live a better life.
- There are storms God sends for our own good.
- Let God have his way with you: you will be a better person.
- God uses suffering to impart wisdom.
- God is teaching us the genuineness of our relationship with Him.
- Could it be that God is trying to get you to stop being evil, selfish, and nasty in order to change?
- God never sends us more burdens than we can bear. Therefore, God knows you can handle the suffering you are experiencing.
- Rejoice, she's in God's hands now!
- We suffer so that we will be more open to mentally and the physically disabled persons.
- Why is God so mean? I thought God was a God of love.
- God in the Old Testament is a God of wrath, but in the New Testament God is a God of Love.
- Why does God punish us after we have been forgiven?
- The devil made me do it!
- The devil is our enemy!
- The devil brought this disease to me.
- I didn't do it; she did it!
- People are their own worst enemy!
- Be careful, you could hurt someone!
- He only did it to himself.
- War is hell!
- These people will never learn.
- People can be so evil.
- Why are people so evil?
- Some people can't see for themselves what's good for them.

- This will hurt me more than it will hurt you!
- Will we ever learn?
- It just happened! It was an accident.
- There are some things you just have to accept.
- There's nothing you can do; just take it.
- You are predestined to suffer.
- We can grow from our pain.
- There are no answers about suffering.
- It's a mystery.

That's quite a list of responses. There might be others you can add. Some of these responses to suffering seem like shouts. Some try to apply reason. Others exhort. Some give up trying to make sense of suffering and decide there are no adequate answers to suffering.

Instead of simply cringing at the exclamations and explanations, I have decided to write a response to suffering.

SUMMARY OF CHAPTER ONE
VOICES

The chapter begins with a list of exclamations, complaints, questions, and possible answers to human suffering. Which one of them do you say most often? Why?

Does your exclamation, question, or answer come from experience, or did you learn it from someone in particular?

A complete class discussion about these and many other questions is available in the Leader's Guide/Discussion Guide.

CHAPTER TWO

DIRECTION

Many people begin their investigation of suffering in the dust of the earth, the material, because the hurt is grounded in the earthiness of the finite human being. Likewise, reasoning, reactions, and questions about suffering almost always begin with the personal experience of a hurtful event and push up and out. The cry of the suffering person is one of "poor me, poor me!" From there, there seems no place to go and nothing to do except shout into the sky "Foul!" Suffering is often a mystery never solved. No matter what we think or feel, suffering continues to be around us and can break into our lives at anytime.

In response to such suffering, there are at least two postures:

1. The suffering one shakes a clenched fist in the night, blows out a candle, and curses God.
2. The suffering one falls to the earth, first on their knees, then prostrate in the dust. Face down, the suffering one covers her eyes with her hands and whispers, "God . . . ."

In both instances, words fly upward into the air. From some we hear shouts: "We are being used and abused, God don't you care?" From others we hear a whisper: "Is there any hope?"

The words float upward. They stop in mid-air. The silence is deafening. Either God does not hear, or the pleas never reach him. It seems that there is no answer for hurt from the earth.

I think there is another answer. That answer is leaven from heaven: I choose to look heavenward. I remind myself that God creates and loves each person. God lifts us up to see, realize, and find purpose in what happens. God says,

- "First, look at me!"
- "Let me help you with answers."
- "Know me from my messages in history."
- "Take a look at what I do and what I have done."
- "I will give you a way to find some answers to what mystifies you."

So I begin with three constants in the Bible that are descriptive of God. We will hold God to them. Only in such certainty and constancy of God can we find answers about suffering. Rather than reasoning upwards from the hurt of the earth, we will reason downwards from the leaven of heaven. For God produces a gracious and transforming influence that explains the purposes of creation and life.

The constants that God reveals for our examination are:

- God is love.
- God is one.
- God is just.

SUMMARY OF CHAPTER TWO
DIRECTIONS

This chapter gives us some basis from which to think about suffering. The cries often go in the direction of "the hurt from the earth" to "leaven from heaven." But it is exactly this God who can give us help and understanding. Science can also help us with understanding. Together God and science can begin a new way of reasoning about pain and suffering. A foundation is set for further questioning and further discovery. There seem to be three pillars or constants that can be deduced about God and Creation: God is love, God is one, and God is just.

A DIRECTION FOR THINKING:

Can God help us to understand suffering? How?

CHAPTER THREE

GOD IS LOVE [THE FIRST CONSTANT]

1 John 4:8 bluntly reminds us that "God is love" (NIV). This reminder is everywhere in the Bible, beginning with the creation story. Who's involved in creation? Only God is involved. From the very beginning we see a loving God who creates everything. God even creates human beings.

From scripture texts like Genesis 1:1, "In the beginning, God created the heavens and the earth" (NIV) and John 3:16, "For God so loved the world . . ." (NIV), we cannot but extrapolate that if God so loved the world, then God loves the universe. Out of love, God creates a multi-faceted universe. From Gods' loving nature comes the creation of all things. We marvel at creation. And why not?

James Irwin, U.S. astronaut, spoke these words about seeing the earth from space:

> The earth reminded us of a Christmas tree ornament hanging in the blackness of space. As we got farther and farther away it diminished in size. Finally, it shrank to the size of a marble, the

most beautiful marble you can imagine. That beautiful warm, living object looked so fragile, so delicate, that if you touched it with a finger it would crumble and fall apart. Seeing this has to change a man, has to make a man appreciate the creation of God and the love of God.[1]

Out of love comes beauty that brings wonderment.

We all realize that God is bigger than our minds and any part of our bodies, but we use human words to speak about God. We hear about God creating with his fingers and God speaking words. We dare to use human body parts when we think of God. It is the only way we have to describe an active God. Could I ask: Am I in God? And is God in me? In creation it seems so. But this universe is fine-tuned to allow life of all kinds, as Sharon Begley reminds us in *The Hand of God*.[2]

A second sort of cosmological discovery can also be interpreted in a way that supports belief. This is the finding that if the laws of physics were tweaked even slightly, the world as we see it would not exist. With just tiny changes in the values of some of the numbers that go into the laws, no one would be around to marvel and wonder at any of this. The cosmos seems fine-tuned for existence, in an almost-too-good-to-be-true manner. To some, this *fine-tuning* of the laws that govern the universe is no less than proof of a designer. Out of love God makes a universe that is not out of control.

> In the beginning when God created the heavens and the earth, the earth was a formless void and covered the face of the deep, while a wind from God swept over the face of the waters. Then God said, 'Let there be light'; and there was light. (Genesis 1:1-3, NRSV)

The Hebrew denotes absolute and total chaos. The wind is the worst storm imaginable. Only God can love enough to turn such a chaotic mess into ordered creation. Many times God says, "Let there be . . . ." And so the ordering begins. The mess is divided and reworked to

---

[1] Michael Reagan, Ed., *The Hand of God,* Andrews McMeel Publishing, 1999, p. 16.
[2] *The Hand of God*, p. 152.

provide a living space for new creations that support human beings. Such love is demonstrated first in the Bible. "So God creates humankind," (Gen 1:27 NRSV). And because creation is one of God's greatest gifts of love to humankind we shall see the chaos of birth lead to ordered life. Physicist Bernard Haish in his book, *The God Theory*[3] stated:

> Some scientists, however, are beginning to recognize how very finely tuned the laws of physics must be to make our existence possible. Take, for instance, British Astronomer Royal, Sir Martin Rees. In his book, *Just Six Numbers*, Rees presents cogent arguments that a mere six numbers determine the nature of our universe. These numbers, which specify the strengths of physical constants, such as the ratio of gravitational to electrical attraction, define the very fabric of our material reality. If their values were slightly different, Rees maintains, life would not be possible here.

What a loving God we have in creating the universe! Our creation has chemical and physical properties that are defined with purpose. They have boundaries that define them. They have purpose not only for creating but also for setting limits that allow human life. These rules for creating are firm. Without these rules, nothing of matter could settle down and be something or someone. Creation is a loving gift of God.

All the laws of nature have worked their way to sustaining life. Our planet and atmosphere have worked just like they should. Our planet is trustworthy.

What if nature were fickle and unpredictable? Suppose summer would continue until all fields were parched or winter stayed so long that all food failed? What if rivers ceased to run? What if one day you have raspberries and the next day poison berries? What would we do if gravity were uneven or stopped all together? Indeed, "A library of gratitude could be written on the fidelities of nature."[4]

---

3 *The God Theory*, Red Wheel, Weiser LLC, 2006, p. 63.
4 George Buttrick, *God, Pain, and Evil*, Abingdon Press, 1966, p. 42.

God has delivered a dependable world. There are extremes that happen, but they are a part of the system. We must work around them and that's what human beings have done for centuries. That's why human beings are adaptable. Even now there are people who are looking for ways to deflect large asteroids that may be heading for a collision with the earth. The rules of nature are closely tethered. Within nature there may be ways to change the course of events. This is similar to a person just leaving town when a hurricane is approaching. We adapt. There are some people who choose not to adapt and they take the risk of severe consequences. God allows room for plants and animals to evolve, but they evolve or adapt within the limits and scope of physics and chemistry.

There are times, in history, when something happens that is a mystery. Somehow an event has occurred but we can not understand how or why it has taken place. It seems to go against the laws of physics. Could God or would God stretch the boundaries so that something could happen out of the ordinary realm of nature? I think not. But there may be things that do appear to break the rules of a fine-tuned universe, but really do not do so.

These following two stories illustrate that the God of love still reaches down to help us as we live in this world. The first story is a preface for the second one.

> One summer evening I was observing our cat, Baby. She was sitting in the hallway where our tall grandfather clock stands. The clock began to strike 10 o'clock. Our cat looked up in wonderment and confusion. She sat and listened. She had absolutely no idea what a clock was or what a clock did. All she heard was a clang, clang, clang.
>
> You see, in *Catdom*, the knowledge of clocks is beyond their brain power. "As long as it does not jump out and chase me, I'm safe," says the cat. The cat will never be able to understand about the clock ticking or striking. It is beyond her creation. Often what happens in *Humandom* is so far advanced that she just cannot ever understand it. The world of *Catdom* is limited. Could this also be

true of human beings as we view miracles? Maybe there is a way for God to lovingly reach down into our world to aid and assist without stretching nature's rules.

* * * * *

Once upon a time a dog came home to his master. He came in, went to a corner, and lay down. At some place and at some time something sharp had cut the dog's paw.

Now, left all alone there is nothing the dog in *Doggygdom* could do for himself except lick the wound and hope the saliva would help the healing. The dog could only rely on a natural healing within *Doggydom*. After the accident, he may have communicated with other dogs about the healing of cuts, scratches, and even worse. They would have all agreed that the tool for healing in *Doggydom* is to lick the wound. That would be the end of their knowledge about healing.

The dog's master noticed that his pet was secluded behind a chair. It was odd behavior for his active, loving dog. So upon inspection, he noticed the dog's wound. He lovingly packed his dog into the car and drove off to the vet. Of course, the veterinarian looked at the wound, cleaned it of germs, put in a few stitches, applied a topical ointment and a bandage and sent the dog home. A wonderful recovery was to take place because someone of the human world reached down and intervened in *Doggydom*. The pet did not understand what took place, with all the procedures, the stitches, and the need for a covering on his paw. He just trusted the love of his master.

Did you realize the injury and the licking, as well as the stitches and the bandage, were all within the creation God gave us? No rules of nature were broken or stretched. The worlds of humans and dogs were allowed to intersect within the one creation. No rules of nature were broken. Notice the dog could not understand what was going on outside of his *Doggydom*. He was blessed!

Could there be ways that God can and does bless us with aids outside of *Humandom*? Are there procedures and aids that God delivers that we do not see or know about? To help us in these ways, God would break no laws of nature. There would exist some higher knowledge than we humans could comprehend, perhaps some of God's special helps, that appear as miracles, work, within this creation's boundaries but in ways that we do not understand.

Who are we as human beings to assume we can have all the answers about life within the universe? Well we don't. Yes, God is love.

One of the greatest signs of God's love is the wonder of making all creations ordered to prevent utter chaos. And the next sign of love from God is the reaching down to us to be present in our lives.

SUMMARY OF CHAPTER THREE
THE FIRST CONSTANT: GOD IS LOVE

Out of love God creates. There are some really "big" rules that have to remain constant if the universe is to stay intact. The chapter gives us some assurance that the world and the universe are not disorganized or accidental. They are ordered!

God works with a structure of order. See Genesis 1.

What look like exceptions to the rules are not exceptions. What look like miracles are God's ways of loving us within the structure, but we are not sure how that happens.

A DIRECTION FOR THINKING:

Which would be better, a creation in chaos or a creation with order? How might that happen?

CHAPTER FOUR

GOD IS JUST [THE SECOND CONSTANT]

Here is another constant that tells us what God does, how he acts, and how he demonstrates his very nature: God is just!

This statement is the same as when someone says, "God is righteous." It means God always does what is right. This is pure justice.

Remember, to understand suffering we must get some foundational biblical statements about God. To understand that God is just, let us begin with Genesis 18:25. God and Abraham are considering what will happen to the city of Jericho if they cannot find fifty righteous persons in order to save all of the people of the city from a fiery judgment. Abraham speaks, "Shall not the judge of all the earth do what is just [or right]?"

We turn to Deuteronomy 32:3 for the next statement:

> I will proclaim the name of the Lord.
> Oh, praise the greatness of our God!
> He is the Rock, his works are perfect,
> and all his ways are *just*.
> A faithful God, who does no wrong,
> *just* and upright is he. (NIV)

The words come directly from the mouth of Moses. The point is made. God is absolutely just.

A third statement about God is written in Psalm 92:14-15. The psalmist is saying that righteous people will be like a fruitful tree:

> They will still bear fruit in old age,
> They will stay fresh and green,
> proclaiming, "The Lord is upright;
> he is my Rock, and there is no injustice in him."

A fourth statement is written in Isaiah 45:21:

> There is no other god besides me,
> a just God and a Saviour,
> there is no one besides me. (NIV)

To begin to get answers about suffering, this constant or just God must be etched into your mind. God is a just God . . . constantly.

SUMMARY OF CHAPTER FOUR
THE SECOND CONSTANT: GOD IS JUST

In this chapter you learn about the existence of another constant that never varies: God is just!

Sometimes the cries of the hurting are hurled up towards heaven. (See Chapters 1 and 2.) They say, "God has brought my suffering" or "It is God's will." So how do we undo the damage done by saying "God is unjust?"

Here are some new thoughts to initiate the struggle to see God as God claims: "I am just, always."

A DIRECTION FOR THINKING:

If God is just, how will God act in this world and in the universe? What does it mean to be perfectly just?

CHAPTER FIVE

GOD IS ONE [THE THIRD CONSTANT]

Let us turn to Deuteronomy 32:39:

> See now that I, even I am he;
> there is no God beside me.

Now Isaiah 45:5-6:

> I am The Lord, and there is no other;
> apart from me there is no god.
> I strengthen you, though you have not acknowledged me.
>
> So that they may know, from the rising of the sun and from the
>   west, that there is no one besides me;
> I am The Lord and there is no other. (NIV)

All these passages insist that God (Yahweh) is one God. This monotheistic mantra is basic theology for the Jews and for Christians. Suppose I asked you, "Do you believe that God is the only God?" I would expect you to say a resounding Yes! Sometime later in this book I will point out that you have changed your initial stance and have compromised your religion. But for now, I want you to hold on to your affirmation about God being one as tightly as you may hold onto the belief of the resurrection of Jesus. Stay strong in monotheism, because later in this book you will be seriously challenged to see that you have indeed abandoned monotheism for another belief. Now onward:

Because there is only one God, the earliest Jews held to a unique theology. If God is one, then all actions seen coming from heaven are from God's hand. This is the oldest of the stances about one God. It caused no end of trouble.

Look at Deuteromony 32:39, especially the second half of this verse:

> See now that I, even I am he; there is no god beside me. I kill and I make alive; I wound and I heal, and no one can deliver from my hand. (NIV)

Now look at Isaiah 45:7. Do you see that the one God does both things, gives life and destroys it, forms both light and darkness, and brings both prosperity and disaster?

Look at Hosea 6:1-2:

> Come let us return to the Lord, for it is he who has torn, and he
>   will heal us;
> he has struck down and he will bind us up.
>
> After two days he will revive us;
>   on the third day he will raise us up,
> that we may live before him. (NRSV)

This passage in Hosea makes a big point. It is a call from God to repent: "For when you do wrong, God will punish you. Yes, God might strike us down; but, then God might nurse us back to health."

It seems that a belief in a monotheistic God in its earliest theology had to allow God to have two sides of action—in this case, kill and make alive. Since there were no other Gods, this one God "Yahweh" apparently did both good and evil. Another way to see it is that all kinds of actions that were unexplainable on earth were accredited to the one God. How else could they view it if there was only one God?

This earliest of theologies gave the Jews nightmares. In certain cases, a voice from Earth could yell, and scream, "God, you're not fair! You're not just!" and in certain cases the voice from suffering was correct.

In the earliest of days, there was no answer but to trust God. However, the Jews would look for a new answer—and they would discover one!

SUMMARY OF CHAPTER FIVE
THE THIRD CONSTANT: GOD IS ONE

The biblical declaration of God's constancy is in Deuteronomy 6:4-9 (God is one). This chapter explores how a monotheistic (one) God was seen in comparison to the many gods of the nations surrounding Israel.

In the earliest of times, the Jews' thinking was very similar to their neighbors'. The neighboring gods could do both good and evil deeds toward their people. And the one God of Israel could do both good and evil toward the people of the land. These actions did not bother Israel for some time, and then finally someone noticed and said, "How can that be? Our one God must not be just. How can our one God pass out evil and good and still be just?"

A real dilemma ensued. A new way of thinking would have to evolve that would see God as Just. We cannot go against the constant "God is just." Therefore, God cannot be seen to give out evil. Period. The Jewish theologians would find a new way of thinking.

A DIRECTION FOR THINKING:

What is the contradiction when the one just God seems to create suffering and then heals it? What about if God kills and yet makes alive?

CHAPTER SIX

A NEW ANSWER, A NEW THEOLOGY

With the dual functions of a monotheistic God, it would seem that God brings pain, burdens, and suffering! This is exactly what drove the Jews to look in yet another direction. For God to bring suffering on all, even the totally innocent, would be a terrible indictment upon a loving, just God. It would mean, in fact, that God would not be loving, or just. God still might be one; but God would not be loving or just. If this predicament could not be altered by another way of thinking, then all the accusations about God in that long list in Chapter One would be valid. As we move on, we will find answers to invalidate all those accusations to God about suffering.

Ultimately, the dual function of God would be focused in another direction.

Wait, the Jews reasoned. God does not indiscriminately send pain or suffering. No, there is a good reason why God sends misfortune: Didn't God save all the Israelites who ventured out of Egypt into the desert? Didn't Israel have the first Passover, and didn't the Pharaoh urge the Israelite captives to leave Egypt? How many times was it said that God would save the people? And God did! And who saved the people who found their direction of flight to be halted by water, only to provide the way out to dry land and freedom? It was God! Did God save some of the people or did God save all the people? Here we have a loving, just God, who acts morally. But how did the people respond to God's love? Some of the people grumbled, instigated revolution and chaos, and worshiped other gods (idols).

They did not respond morally or right to this God who just loved them. A just and moral God desires that his people will be just, moral, and loving back to Him. Instead of loving God, they took God for granted. They did not appreciate their freedom. Everything around them was not the way they wanted it. So the people rejected God. They turned their backs on Him. They acted immorally without love; and they grumbled all the way along.

How would or should a just God respond to a people who ignored God? He asked for moral actions, and the people acted with grumbling, hatred, and violence. He asked for exclusive loyalty, and the people renewed idol worship.

This is what God did. God said, "I have been good to you; and you have shunned me. Therefore, I am going to hold you responsible to your early promises to me. I will try to get you back by asking you to return, to change direction, and come back. If you will not return because you love me, I will be totally just and allow hardships to come your way. And maybe then you will turn back and follow me."

A new theology was born: If you do good, good things will happen to you. If you do bad, bad things will happen to you. This was the new theology that evolved out of the ancient monotheistic God, who seemed to be indiscriminately just and unjust at the same time.

Restated: Now God will bless those who act morally with good will and have a relationship with Him. But God will punish those who act immorally with evil intentions and turn from their relationship with Him.

This theology would hold for a long time. In fact, even today this theology has many in its grip because they have been taught that it is true and they believe it to be true.

But a day would come when this theology would be replaced because of its imperfections.

Example: How many people, in hanging picture frames on the wall, have missed the nail with the hammer and pounded their own fingers and shouted, "Ouch! What did I ever do to deserve that?" This theology is still alive today.

But do *you* still believe it? Do you still believe:

> Do good; receive goodness. Do bad; receive evil.

So for the Jews, the new answer is in Deuteronomy 32:3-5 especially verse 5:

> For I will proclaim the name of the Lord;
> ascribe greatness to our God!
> The Rock, his work is perfect, and all his ways are just.
> A faithful God, without deceit, just and upright is he;
> yet his degenerate children have dealt falsely with him, a perverse
> and crooked generation. (NRSV)

So now it is reprobate human beings who cause troubles to come to themselves and to the earth. Human beings are now held responsible! The reason for suffering is now ascribed to *sinners*. Remember the phrase, "Ouch! What did I ever do to deserve this?" Now you know from where that thinking comes.

Now we arrive at the Book of Job. The answer to get God off the hot seat is that human beings cause trouble for themselves. They are sinners and therefore deserve pain, suffering, and problems as retribution for sin.

As you read the opening verses of Job, remember the theology:

> Do good; receive goodness. Do bad; receive evil.

A BOOK OF WISDOM

JOB 1:1-5

> There was once a man in the land of Uz whose name was Job. That man was blameless and upright, one who feared God and turned away from evil. There were born to him seven sons and three daughters. He had seven thousand sheep, three thousand camels, five hundred yoke of oxen, five hundred donkeys, and very many servants; so that this man was the greatest of all the people of the east. His sons used to go and hold feasts in one another's houses in turn: and they would send and invite their three sisters to eat and drink with them. And when the feast days had run their course, Job would send and sanctify them, and he would rise early in the morning and offer burnt offerings according to the number of them all; for Job said, "It may be that my children have sinned, and cursed God in their hearts." (NRSV)

(Notice this is what Job always did.)

COMMENTARY:

Chapter 1: Shows us a man (a human being). His name is Job.

The author identifies Job with not just one or two or three but four descriptions. He is:

> 1. Blameless; 2. upright; 3. one who feared God; 4. one who turned away from evil. In short, he is pure in all respects.

If we hold with the theology of the day, that if one does good, one receives goodness, and if one does evil, one receives evil, then Job clearly deserved good to come to him. (And it did. Go back and read vv. 2-5.)

But before long, Job will suffer beyond description. No wonder Job will lift his head toward heaven and say, "I don't deserve this stuff. According to the theology, I should never have to suffer!"

What Job did not know was what God and one heavenly being on the council of God were talking about. This being was the district attorney for God accusing people on the earth with sin and error. His name was Satan. The conversation is recorded in 1:6-12. God asks Satan what he has observed about Job and his blamelessness and goodness.

JOB 1:6-12

> One day the heavenly beings came to present themselves before the Lord, and Satan also came among them. The Lord said to Satan, "Where have you come from?" Satan answered the Lord, "From going to and fro on the earth, and from walking up and down on it." The Lord said to Satan, "Have you considered my servant Job? There is no one like him on the earth, a blameless and upright man who fears God and turns away from evil." Then Satan answered the Lord, "Does Job fear God for nothing? Have you not put a fence around him and his house and all that he has, on every side? You have blessed the work of his hands, and his possessions have increased in the land. But stretch out your hand now, and touch all that he has, and he will curse you to your face." The Lord said to Satan, "Very well, all that he has is in your power; only do not stretch out your hand against him!" (NRSV) So Satan went out from the presence of the Lord.

COMMENTARY:

In verse 9, Satan makes an accusation because he knows Job is human:

> Why should Job not be good, you have protected him, you have blessed him beyond measure (my paraphrase).

I cannot understand why Satan was ignorant of the new theology. God was doing exactly what was called for. Good things for good people. Satan said, "Give him some trouble and he will curse you." So God and his district attorney make a gentleman's bet. But poor Job will get the suffering, in order to settle a point.

JOB 1:13-22

Now read verses 13-22. Destruction and woe will come to Job. But Job will not curse God.

> One day when his sons and daughters were eating and drinking wine in the eldest brother's house, a messenger came to Job and said, "The oxen were plowing and the donkeys were feeding beside them, and the Sabeans fell on them and carried them off, and killed the servants with the edge of the sword. I alone have escaped to tell you." While he was still speaking, another came and said, "The fire of God fell from heaven and burned up the sheep and the servants, and consumed them; I alone have escaped to tell you." While he was still speaking, another came and said, "The Chaldeans formed three columns, made a raid on the camels and carried them off, and killed the servants with the edge of the sword; I alone have escaped to tell you." While he was still speaking, another messenger came and said, "Your sons and daughters were eating and drinking wine in their eldest brother's house, and suddenly a great wind came across the desert, struck the four corners of the house, and it fell on the young people, and they are dead; I alone have escaped to tell you." Then Job rose, tore his robe, shaved his head, and fell on the ground and worshiped. He said, "Naked I came from my mother's womb, and naked shall I return there; the Lord gave and the Lord has taken away: blessed be the name of the Lord." In all this Job did not sin or charge God with wrong doing. (NRSV)

JOB 2:1-10

In Job 2:1 ff., the attack on Job's health continues, and a second conversation occurs.

> One day the heavenly beings came to present themselves before the Lord, and Satan also came among them to present himself before the Lord. The Lord said to Satan, "Where have you come from?" Satan answered the Lord, "From going to and fro on the earth, and from walking up and down on it." The Lord said to Satan, "Have you considered my servant Job? There is no one like him on the earth, a blameless and upright man who fears God and turns away from evil. He still persists in his integrity, although you incited me against him, to destroy him for no reason." Then Satan answered the Lord, "Skin for skin! All that people have they will give to save their lives, but stretch out your hand now and touch his bone and his flesh, and he will curse you to your face." The Lord said to Satan, "Very well, he is in your power; only spare his life." So Satan went out from the presence of the Lord, and inflicted loathsome sores on Job from the sole of his foot to the crown of his head. Job took a potsherd with which to scrape himself, and sat among the ashes. Then his wife said to him, "Do you still persist in your integrity? Curse God, and die." But he said to her, "You speak as any foolish woman would speak. Shall we receive the good at the hand of God, and not receive the bad?" In all this Job did not sin with his lips. (NRSV)

COMMENTARY:

Did you notice that Chapter 2:1-6 mirrors Chapter 1:6-12?

This time God allows Satan to take away Job's own health. The suffering becomes greater and greater. This situation is worse than any human being has ever suffered. It is deliberately presented this way. What person today could be so devastated?

In verse 9, Job's wife encourages him to curse God. It's not supposed to be this way! she seems to say. But still Job will not curse God.

Check out these points:

- Job is virtually sinless and still he suffers.
- This book is a piece of Wisdom Literature that tells a story to challenge the theology of the day.
- The Book of Job is a test case only. It is a story composed to show the deficits of the theology. Do good—receive good; Do bad—receive evil. Here a good man is getting bad things. It should not be happening this way! Can the theology stand up to such a rigorous examination and challenge?

Many people today go to Job for help in their sufferings. They say, "I'm suffering like Job—poor me!"

Listen! We have absolutely nothing in common with Job! Job is perfect in his humanness. We are not. He is suffering far worse than any human. We are not in his league. This book was written to demonstrate the inadequacy of the then current theology.

Next, some friends of Job come to visit him one after another offering the current theological answers.

JOB 8:1-7

In Job 8:1-7, Bildad speaks to Job.

> Then Bildad the Shuite answered. "How long will you say these things, and the words of your mouth be a great wind? Does God pervert justice? Or does the Almighty pervert the right? If your children sinned against him, he delivered them into the power of their transgression. If you will seek God and make supplication to the Almighty, if you are pure and upright, surely then he will rouse himself for you and restore to you your rightful place. Though your beginning was small your latter days will be very great." (NRSV)

COMMENTARY:

Bildad lays it down: "You must have sinned to have so much trouble. Repent!"

JOB 5:6-7

In Job 5:6-7, a friend called Eliphaz visits Job and tells him:

> "For misery does not come from the earth, nor does trouble sprout from the ground; but human beings are born to trouble, just as sparks are born to fly upward." (NRSV)

COMMENTARY:

Here Eliphaz tells Job to go back to school. We have been taught that misery comes from sin not from the earth. Boy, can we hear the present theology sound here: Misery is the result of human sinning. That is the answer, Job— You hurt because you sinned."

JOB 5:17-18

> Eliphaz continues, "How happy is the one whom God reproves; therefore do not despise the discipline of the Almighty. For he wounds but he binds up; he strikes but his hand heals." (NRSV)

COMMENTARY:

Do you hear it? "Job, it is in response to your sins that God punishes you. Repent, and he will heal you."

So where does suffering come from? Some ask, "Does it come from a righteous God who responds to sin with justice and truth?" *No!* "Is punishment and hardship God's way of getting you back to Him?" *No!* Misery is the result of sin and certainly not from God. God is righteous. Human beings are the reason for pain and suffering.

But Job retorts, "What have I done wrong? Show me. I have done no evil, so why is there suffering?" Good Question!

The Book of Job attacks innocent suffering. Job says, "I am innocent and yet I suffer. Something is wrong here!"

This theology is an inadequate reality. It does not accurately describe all circumstances. Therefore, this theology fails.

The place where this theology fails is that the Jews read the sayings in a backward direction. To do it *for*ward would entail the following:

Do good, and watch good happen to you. Do bad, and watch evil happen to you.

Reading this theology (forward) is often truthful isn't it? For example,

> A. Everyone in prison is receiving punishment for sin.
> B. When your child puts a hand on the hot plate, the sound that is heard is, ouch! because of the burn.
> C. Even if you are not caught for a sin, guilt and shame will pull you down.

In those days, the scholars and population began to read it backwards. For example,

> I see prosperity in him; therefore he must be sinless and good.

Or,

> I see disease and suffering in her; therefore she is nothing but a sinner.

This theology fails because reading backwards is ludicrous. Is all prosperity because of goodness? Is all suffering because of doing evil? Nonsense.

Job was clearly written to smash this theology. Listen: when people get diseases or someone gets hurt or killed, people often yell,

"Why, God?" Today we know in almost all cases why! We can find out through autopsies and examinations why people get diseases or hurt or killed. The reports tell us logically and rationally how this happened and that happened, and how all this progressed to that and bang! Yes, we can find out why people suffer.

What is troubling is when a young lad goes across a field to get home from school and is struck dead by lightning. Why? We know why. The boy was a lightning rod in an empty field. It was no moral fault of his own, but he innocently walked into a law of nature.

"Foul!" we yell. "He did not deserve this! He is an innocent sufferer!" So throw out the old theologies and get me an answer for innocent suffering! We see that Job is an innocent sufferer just like the little boy!

So Job asks for an audience with God, and he gets one.

Job claims he is innocent.

No comment comes from God.

JOB 38:1-2

God speaks, "Who is this that babbles on? I have had it with you. You are a human being."

COMMENTARY:

Paraphrasing, what God is saying here is, "Now I'll ask the questions."

Job 40:2 (God speaks) "Shall a fault finder contend with the Almighty?" (NRSV)

Listen, even if Job were perfect, he would still not be God but a created one of a Holy God.

JOB 40:6

Job goes on to admit he is just a puny human being.

God says in verse 40:6, "Will you (Job) put me in the wrong that you may be justified?"

COMMENTARY:

In other words, God asks, "Will you make me out to be in the wrong when you suffer, in order to be justified?"

Listen, when we suffer it is an option to look around and find someone to blame—even God! As Zig Zigler would say, "That's stinken thinkin'!"

Finally, after the exchanges with God, Job is justified. But God asks, "Who dares blame me, a Holy God?" That is the issue. And we answer, "No one Lord God, we are but puny humans."

No real answer for innocent suffering is offered. God pulls rank. Job is not God, but he is justified for his behavior. The theology of the day has great holes in it. Reading it backwards, as Job's friends did, kills the theology. Now the Jews will linger on in history to find a new answer for innocent suffering. They will find one.

But please note: Jesus also puts down this old theology.

LUKE 13:1-5

> At that very time there were some present who told him about the Galileans whose blood Pilate had mingled with their sacrifices. He asked them, "Do you think that because these Galileans suffered in this way they were worse sinners than all other Galileans? No, I tell you; but unless you repent, you will all perish as they did. Or those eighteen who were killed when the tower of Siloam fell on them—do you think that they were worse offenders than all the others living in Jerusalem? No, I tell you; but unless you repent, you will all perish just as they did." (NRSV)

COMMENTARY:

There were two calamities that resulted in deaths. One was a political insurrection and the other was the collapse of a tower named Siloam. The disciples asked if those deaths were due to the dead people's sinfulness? Jesus said, "*No!*" So much for that theology!

JOHN 9:1-3

> As he walked along, he saw a man blind from birth. His disciples asked him, "Rabbi, who sinned, this man or his parents, that he was born blind?" And Jesus answered, "Neither this man nor his parents sinned." (NRSV)

COMMENTARY:

The old theology is dead. Don't try to apply it any more. Anyway, the old theology can never answer the problems of innocent suffering. And the Jews kept searching.

LUKE 16:19-31

> There was a rich man who was dressed in purple and fine linen and who feasted sumptuously every day. And at his gate lay a poor man named Lazarus, covered with sores, who longed to satisfy his hunger with what fell from the rich mans's table; even the dogs would come and lick his sores. The poor man died and was carried away by the angels to be with Abraham. The rich man also died and was buried. In Hades, where he was being tormented, he looked up and saw Abraham far away with Lazarus by his side. He called out, 'Father Abraham, have mercy on me, and send Lazarus to dip the tip of his finger in water and cool my tongue; for I am in agony in these flames.' But Abraham said, 'Child, remember that during your lifetime you received your good things, and Lazarus in like manner evil things; but now is comforted here, and you are in agony. Besides all this, between you and us a great chasm has been fixed, so that those who might want to pass from here to you cannot do so, and no one can cross from there to us.' He said, 'Then, father, I beg you to send him to my father's house—for I have five brothers—that he may warn them, so that they will not also come into this place of torment.' Abraham replied, 'They have Moses and

the prophets; they should listen to them.' He said, 'No, father Abraham; but if someone goes to them from the dead, they will repent.' He said to him, 'If they do not listen to Moses and the prophets, neither will they be convinced even if someone rises from the dead.'" (NRSV)

COMMENTARY:

During their life on earth the rich man lead a sumptuous life, while Lazarus experiences a beggar's life. Both men died. It is in the next conscious existence that these two men find their roles to be reversed. The rich man finds himself in a place of torment as the reward for his life. Lazarus finds himself next to the great patriarch Abraham. It is apparent that in Abraham's presence Lazarus needs absolutely nothing. This is his just reward for his former life of misery.

The theology of the day would say that God blesses the rich man, and that the poor man is a sufferer and therefore a sinner. But this parable says such assumptions are wrong. The old theological formula is totally rejected by God.

Jesus is saying that the arrogant, rich man God does not bless, and that instead God honors the sick man Lazarus.

This old theology will not stand up in the face of innocent suffering. The Jews went into exile looking for a new answer. They found one. However, even in subsequent years the old theology was still around and thought to be true in many people's minds. Even Jesus' undercutting of the old theology did not stop its influence.

Even the Jewish community of our day declares the old theology dead in its tracks. Rabbi Morton M. Applebaum of Temple Israel, Akron, Ohio in *What Everyone Should Know about Judaism*[1] answers a hundred questions with wonderfully succinct answers. One question was, "Why are Jews such a Persecuted People?" I will quote about half of the answer, and it will call to question the theology illustrated so vehemently in Job:

---

1 Emwa Books, 1978, pp. 26, 28.

This question smacks of an antiquated belief in divine retributive justice which conceives of 'good for good' and 'bad for bad'. According to such thinking, the persecution of Jews throughout the ages must be proof of the punishment that fits the crime, God-sent suffering for Jewish sinfulness. This is the very point of view with which the Book of Job comes to grips and repudiates. The three friends contend that Job's misfortunes are manifestations of guilt and divine displeasure. But in the epilogue of the Book, God vindicates Job and condemns the friends' irrational belief in such divine retributive justice. What is true of the individual holds good for a people. What persecution the Jewish people has suffered can neither be attributed to God nor be considered punishment for sinfulness. To imply that the recent liquidation of six million Jews by the Nazis was the will of God would be to impeach His goodness and to absolve the murderers of any guilt. It would be to accept any and all forms of persecution as divine intent, and absolve all persecutors. This is not reasonable."

Isn't it interesting that for all the rejection of this theology of retributive justice, our world certainly tries to keep a hold of it in some manner? But no matter how long the world holds onto it, the old theology will never adequately give an answer for the justification of sufferings and hurts. The Jews did indeed find another answer.

SUMMARY OF CHAPTER SIX
A NEW ANSWER, A NEW THEOLOGY

This chapter explores the revelation of a new theology that seems just. But this theology has problems, too. This theology is the Deuteronomic understanding about God's actions. The consequences of irresponsibility fall on the shoulders of human beings who do wrong, evil deeds. This new way of thinking allows God to be just on both sides of the theology:

> Do good, get blessings.
> Do bad, get punished.

The chapter shows the shortcoming of this new theology. I call it "reading backwards." This way of thinking cannot hold up to serious questioning.

A DIRECTION FOR THINKING:

Can you describe this new theology? How does it help to get us away from the first theology? (Chapter Five) What problems or weaknesses does the new theology have?

CHAPTER SEVEN

A NEW ANSWER COMES FROM FAR AWAY

We have looked at how the Jews struggled to find answers to suffering. At first, a monotheistic God is seen to do it all. Recall Deuteronomy 32:39: "I bring death and I give life. I wound and I heal." The observation that is so troubling is that God sends suffering.

But wait. This God is supposed to be a perfectly just God. How can such a God send suffering? Justice means perfectly just, meaning God must bless the good and punish the bad.

Now the tables turn. Now human beings determine their future existence by their thoughts and actions. Now suffering is not something that God passes around or gives away. No: by being evil, the person deserves the suffering he or she receives.

But what about the innocent ones who suffer? They do not deserve to suffer. What about the system that cannot answer the question: "Why do innocents suffer?" We must look elsewhere for an answer. And in Babylon we find a new answer.

In 587 BCE, the Babylonians swept through Palestine and destroyed Jerusalem. The exiles went to live in the east in Babylonia. Polytheistic peoples lived around the Jews for hundreds of years. But up to this time, the Jews had not seriously considered taking a good look at "many" Gods as a part of a new, accepted Pantheon. Zoroastrianism was well established by the time the Jews arrived in the east. The Jews were introduced to the grand structures of multiple gods. There were hierarchies of gods of differing types. We call this structure dualism. Dualism has a large organized group of "good gods" and a large organized group of "evil Gods." Under the evil gods category there were miniature "little gods" called demons. And under the good gods there were "angels." Such dualism was not unknown to the Jews, but now in such dire straits of exile, they might ask, "Is there something we are missing in not understanding the divine operating on two levels called dualism?"

Obviously, they believed so.

The Supreme God in Zoroastrianism was Ahura Mazda. The chief evil god was Ahiram. The exiled Jews began to look for a corresponding god for each category. It was not long before the accepted answer was that Yahweh God was the Supreme God, and that Satan was the chief Demon of evil.

In 538 BCE when the first of the exiles began to return home to Israel, guess what they brought along with them? They brought along a dualistic hierarchy with two gods doing battle with one another: The good God Yahweh and the bad divine presence of Satan. In the minds of the people, this was the perfect solution to the question, "Why do innocent people suffer?" Later, the word *Devil* would and could be interchanged with the word *Satan*. Both words described the top evil presence challenging Yahweh. By the time of Jesus, most Jews had accepted this dualism as part of daily life. Only the most conservative Jews and Sadducees would not accept this new way of belief.

Now read carefully here. I do not believe in the presence or reality of the Devil or Satan. Along with growing numbers of pastors, teachers, and scholars around the globe, I reject this belief. I do not believe that innocent people suffer because of the Devil. I do not accept this idea, which comes from nothing more than a pagan religion or pagan religions. I believe that the hierarchies of all other religions were and are still idols from the past. They do not exist in reality, only in our imaginations. I do not believe that a devil is on the loose hurting people whether guilty of sin or innocent of sin. For me that is a non-answer.

The next chapter will include a more detailed explanation of how I came to my conclusions.

For many Jews and Christians the devil is indeed the answer for why people suffer and do wicked things. For me it is no answer. I just do not believe in the presence of a pagan God nor in a personified devil.

If the devil is accepted as an answer, then the world and society is in complete turmoil. Evil is on every side, and in every spot. Everyone is vulnerable to massive negative forces on the outside pushing inward to possess or "run" the lives of everyone. Where is God now? If there are devils and demons everywhere, then this coupled with our nature, "to sin," is a predicament beyond description. In Jesus' day, the Jews were captive to Roman occupation. That was evil. Then there was the daily human temptation to sin. And next there were the pressures of demons and devils attacking you, hurting you, giving disease, and starting accidents. Wow, what a mess! Life was hard. Who can help us? Surely God can help us.

During the intertestamental period, about 250 BCE, a form of literature called apocalyptic began to take form. These writings say that the world is so evil that God will have to save it. He is the only one who has the power to do it. The time is coming.

For the Jew, there was hope in the prophecy of Joel . . . the day of the Lord. Originally, people understood the day of the Lord as negative punishment for sinners by God. By the time of Jesus, it was seen as a positive breaking into history by God to rescue his people. There would be an earthly reign of the Messiah when all enemies, forces of evil, and suffering would be vanquished. There would be a forever victory where God was present with his faithful people.

Christians believed that Jesus, the resurrected Messiah, would return to the earth, defeat God's enemies, smash all the forces of evil, and lead the resurrected faithful to heaven. God would be triumphant and victorious. The Book of Revelation tells us this. It is apocalyptic.

Now, let me fulfill a promise made in an earlier chapter. If you believe in a personified devil or Satan that goes about causing pain, suffering and evil, then you have admitted to believing in two Gods. You have taken an idol from Babylonia and made him a God. You have accepted the worldview of dualism and have placed the devil or Satan as an equal adversary for Yahweh/God. You no longer believe in the first constant of the Jewish religion: "I believe in one God." You now have a dualism with critters everywhere, with the supreme God of evil being the devil.

Think hard on this. The answer of dualism came from far away outside of Judea.

It certainly does answer the question about from where innocent suffering comes from. But, what if the Devil is fiction? What if the Devil is a mere idol created from human imagination? If so, the devil cannot be an answer to suffering in any category. We must, therefore, keep looking for a better answer than blaming the devil for all our woes, pains, and suffering.

[Note: This chapter has traced the passage by which the devil (Satan) had become the answer for unexplainable suffering. My extra commentary about the devil, real or unreal, is not the purpose here. If you read Chapter 8, please use it as additional information and not as the central purpose of this book.]

SUMMARY OF CHAPTER SEVEN
A NEW ANSWER COMES FROM FAR AWAY

This chapter shows how the Jews in Babylonian exile experienced cultural and religious shock, particularly dualism of gods. They learned that there is a consortium of good gods and a consortium of evil gods who oppose each other and constantly battle for supremacy of the spiritual world. There are councils around each primary god. And there is a supreme god of Good and a supreme god of Evil.

The Jews are drawn to believe in a dualism coming into Judaism. A dualism can answer many of the unknowns in Jewish theology. The difficult questions about evil and good can be answered with the presence of a supreme evil god in their hierarchy of Judaism.

The exiles start returning to Israel in 538 BCE. They come home with a new spiritual structure, one that is dualistic. Not all Jewish groups champion this new dualistic theology with Satan as the chief evil god.

A DIRECTION FOR THINKING:

With the introduction of Satan being the presence of evil in a dualistic world, how does this help us understand the presence of innocent suffering in the world?

CHAPTER EIGHT

SATAN

Scholars will tell us that the passages that contain the word Satan in the Old Testament can be separated into those written before the exile and those written after. In fact, there are scholars, like Victor B. Hamilton[1], who will tell you that all of the references to Satan in the Old Testament really mean "accuser," and that at "Nowhere in the Old Testament does Satan appear as a distinctive demonic figure, opposed to God and responsible for all evil." Y. Kaufman, in his book *The Religion of Israel*[2] explains that, "Biblical religion was unable to reconcile itself with the idea that there was a power in the universe that defied the authority of God and that could serve as an antigod, the symbol and source of evil. Hence, it strove to transfer evil from the metaphysical realm to the moral realm, to the realm of sin." In short, it placed evil squarely on the shoulders of human sin, rather than on some divine presence who had power to oppose God.

---

1 *The Anchor Bible Dictionary*, Doubleday, 1992, p. 985.
2 M. Greenburg, transl., University of Chicago Press, 1960, p. 65.

In Job, Satan is only an "accuser" for the council of God and should be seen that way in all of the Old Testament texts where Satan appears or disappears. Satan is merely acting out his job description or function as an "accuser," even if in the book of Zechariah Satan is considered a proper name instead. Zechariah would be counted as a book written after the exile, and therefore written with full knowledge of the importation of exilic dualism and evil Gods.

There is little doubt that the stories written after the exile depict Satan as being nastier. And when the Hebrews began to leave Babylonia for the trip back to Jerusalem, they packed in their bags the ideals and advantages of a dualism of gods. Some scholars believe that these particular ideas came originally from Indian religion. Some of the same demons in Zoroastrianism are called daevas, which is the equivalent of the Indian word *deva* for "sky" god. In short, the Jews returned from exile with pieces of pagan religions, such as Satan and dualism, that they incorporated into their own religion.

Not all Jews accepted this change. The liberal Pharisees did, but a few small orthodox groups, which revered only the Pentateuch (the first five books of the bible), would not go along with this new vision of the spiritual world.

I recall a TV interview at which three men were evaluating the movie *The Exorcist*. One was in full, formal clerical garb; one was in a suit and tie; and one was in a short-sleeved shirt with a tie. The man in short sleeves was leaning with his elbow on the table and his chin on the heel of his hand. He showed distinct disregard for the interview.

The man in clerical garb was a Roman Catholic priest. "Father," the interviewer asked, "does the Roman Catholic Church believe in demon possession?" The priest said, "Of course we do! However, we examine each incident with great care. If we believe that the event was legitimate, we will apply to the correct division at the Vatican and get permission to have an exorcism. The church has liturgies to help drive out the demons."

The interviewer then asked the Presbyterian pastor about his denomination's stance toward demon possession. The pastor replied,

"The Presbyterian Church regards such situations with great reserve and care. We would be very careful to determine what was going on here. We believe that most demon possessions are really psychosomatic or self-induced for some personal reason. We are suspicious of these events; however, we do believe that demon possession is possible."

Then turning to the rabbi, the interviewer asked, "Rabbi Swartz, what is the reaction of orthodox Jewry on this topic?" The man leaning on his elbow looked askance at the other pastors and replied, "What's the big deal? I'm an orthodox rabbi. There is no such thing as the devil in our scriptures! We have none other than one God! There is no power other than God except for human beings. It is all a figment of your imagination!" After that I can remember shouting, "Amen Brother!" I believe in evil, I just don't personify it.

There have been people who believed that suffering came form Satan. St. Paul was one.

II Cor. 12:7-10 (NIV):

> Therefore, in order to keep me from becoming conceited, I was given a thorn in my flesh, a messenger of Satan, to torment me. Three times I pleaded with the Lord to take it away from me. But he said to me, "My grace is sufficient for you, for my power is made perfect in weakness." Therefore I will boast all the more gladly about my weaknesses, so that Christ's power may rest on me. That is why, for Christ's sake, I delight in weaknesses, in insults, in hardships, in persecutions, in difficulties. For when I am weak, then I am strong.

What is important for our study is the reference to the messenger of Satan. Paul saw Satan as an evil purveyor of pain and suffering. Please remember that Paul was a member of the liberal Pharisees.

In our world, there are satanic people. They are not the devil, but they act devilishly. Hitler would be an example. Some think that Hitler was merely insane and out of touch with reality. I think he was insanely evil, but not a messenger from a personified evil. But for many people, Satan is evil personified just like Santa Claus is the personification of joy and happiness.

Many years ago the comedian Flip Wilson would perform a skit dressed as a woman who was easily dissuaded from her principles. Flip Wilson would prance around as Geraldine, walking down the street looking into store windows. In one episode, she finds a red dress that she really wants. She imagines all the reasons why she should not have the dress, but finally she gives in to the temptation. Later, out of the store she prances wearing this bright red dress that shouts, "Wow!" Then she turns toward the camera and exclaims, "The devil made me do it!"

The TV audience howled with laughter—even though nobody really believed it was the action of the devil. It was Geraldine who made the decision. Geraldine might have thought, "If I blame someone else, I will feel better as I prance down the street in my new dress." Finally, everyone across America thought, "Who is she kidding?"

There have always been liberal views of the devil. Those persons who believe in a personified Devil challenged the idea of God as the sole divine presence in the universe and the world.

Jesus ben Sirach in Eccles 21:27 (missing in the Hebrew text) said that, "when an ungodly man curses satan, what he is really cursing is his own self." This passage is rendered in the RSV as: "When an ungodly man curses his adversary, he curses his own soul."

Many people blame Satan for their misdeeds, but this is pure imagination and personification of their own nature and their own desires.

Now, I certainly believe in evil. It comes from the desires and moods of human beings. But please don't join the pagans in personifying the devil or Satan.

Now read about a flip-flop in the Old Testament.

2 Samuel 24:1:

> Again the anger of the Lord kindled against Israel, and he incited David against them, to go and count the people of Israel and Judah. (NRSV)

Note that the text says that the Lord God was the one who prompted the idea of taking a census, and that David responded to that prompting. Later, in vs. 10, we learn that David is struck to the quick for having counted the people. There was a law that said no one was to take a census. David did. But look who was reported to have encouraged wrongdoings: God! Wow!

This writing of Samuel comes from an early tradition written before the exile.

But if we look at I Chronicles 21:1 we read that: "Satan stood up against Israel, and incited David to count the people of Israel. So David said to Joab and the commanders of the army, 'Go, number Israel....'" (NRSV)

I Chronicles was written after the exile. I Samuel reflects the time when God was firmly seen as one God, and a unified God would have to send both sides of encouragement and destruction. Recall God saying, "I kill and I make alive."

So rather than allow this old tradition to confuse people, the writers after the exile, finding "Satan" from another culture, now use him to encourage David. This now speaks backward into history to correct, if you may, the former writing of Samuel. It was written that way then, but now we have a clearer picture of what really happened. We didn't have this information back then. Now we correct when we have more of an answer than before. Another way of seeing this is to say that I Chronicles cleans up David. Their fair-haired King could not be so evil; therefore, to the devil we go to give all the blame.

To say this differently, postexilic scholars could not believe that God would ask a person like David to sin. So they changed views and blamed it on Satan.

We can go to the New Testament to see the same kind of warning to people: "Do not accuse God of sin or of tempting someone to sin." Look at James 1:13 (NRSV):

> No one when tempted should say, "I am being tempted by God"; for God cannot be tempted by evil and he himself tempts no one.

Even New Testament writers could not entertain the idea that God would tempt anyone to sin. That would go against God's very nature. What would be even worse would be to think that God would actually send suffering to people. That would make God completely immoral!

However, there are some people even today who will say that God sends suffering so that people will be drawn to God, or so that human beings will be disciplined or chastened, or so that we learn to be better persons. Some say that the storms God sends are for our own good.

Stop it!

There is no good reason that God will go against his own nature and send suffering or temptation. People should stop creating reasons for God to break his righteousness in order to justify hurting us. God will not send suffering or temptation to sin. At least the scholars selected Satan as an alternative. It is Satan who can bring suffering to people. Satan is seen as evil and fickle. Satan inclines towards actions of hurting, maiming, and killing. Satan is known to work on our human nature to get us to think negatively and then act upon those evil thoughts. But even Jesus will not hold completely to this stance. Jesus will suggest another view, as does the author of James.

In Matthew 15, the Pharisees and lawyers come to Jesus complaining about the disciples not washing their hands before meals as the oral law demands. And off to the races Jesus and the Pharisees go, arguing their points. After the confrontation, Peter says to Jesus, "Tell us what the parable means."

Matthew 15:16:

> Then he said, "Are you also without understanding? Do you not see that whatever goes into the mouth enters the stomach, and goes out into the sewer? But what comes out of the moth proceeds from the heart and this is what defiles. For out of the heart come evil intentions, murder, adultery, fornication, theft, false witness, slander. These are what defile a person, but to eat with unwashed hands does not defile. (NRSV)

Jesus tells Peter (v. 18) that wickedness and evil have their beginnings in the hearts of men and women. All the terrible actions Jesus lists proceed from the heart. These are the things that hurt the world. Jesus never mentions that these deeds come from the devil and neither does the author of James:

> But one is tempted by one's own desire, being lured and enticed by it; then when that desire has conceived, it gives birth to sin, and that sin when it is fully grown, gives birth to death. (James 1:14-15, NRSV)

Now I ask you: where is Satan? As long as human beings are self-centered and decide to live within that small circle, there will be exploitation, hate, revenge, jealousy, scheming, and war.

But thank God there is forgiveness of sin through Jesus Christ, and thank goodness there is another way of thinking and living.

Inevitably, someone in a class at this point will raise an objection: "But Jesus healed people possessed with demons. How can you just wipe away everything he said? It's the word of God!"

Jesus was born into a culture that was well entrenched in a dualism of God and angels, Satan and demons. Those who opposed this point of view were in the minority, as were the Sadducees. They had the power behind the temple institution and the priestly power of sacrifice. They controlled the temple and its worship. The Pharisees had the hearts and minds of the "people." They were more liberal, and their ancestors brought dualism back to Jerusalem from Babylon. Certainly Jesus was familiar with both sides of the issue.

If I were going to take the reader in a flashback to somewhere in history, it would be to Salem and the witch trials. We would sit and watch as a woman was being accused and damned for being a witch. As the trial nears the verdict from the jury, you know that unless someone says something or does something, this woman will die for something we don't think even exists today.

So you get up to speak in that courtroom where everyone believes in witchcraft. You say, "Folks, I come to you from a time 350 years into your future. I am here to tell you that there is no such thing as witches. They do not exist! Nor is there anything real about witchcraft!" How do you think that would fly?

And also dear reader, what do you think they would do to you? You couldn't get out of that building fast enough!

Years ago I experienced the following in a parish in which I was the pastor. Along with his wife and family, George was one of the church members. He was known around the area as someone who was absorbed in witchcraft. One day, I went out to visit George.

We had a long visit together. George was in his seventies. He was hunched over. At one time he had been 6 feet tall, but now he was 5'4" at best. There was a pronounced hump on his bowed back. It was definitely a physical ailment from genetics. We went outside and sat on a concrete retaining wall along the driveway.

He said, "I have a neighbor who is a farmer. I will not tell you who he is or in what direction he lives. He is a witch. He has cursed me. I am possessed by his curse. Look at my back. He has cursed me and my farm and my house."

At that point, George went into his beliefs about the bewitching world in which he lived. For two hours I listened to him. He described evil and how it works. He used scripture from Daniel and Revelation. I got into his words and feelings. I began to be absorbed into his world. It was scary. His mood was dark and present. I was slipping into the time of the Salem witch trials. I could feel the people's fears and worries. George totally pulled me in to the point that I could have said, "I could believe this in a different time and place."

George said, "I fight this witch every day. I'm getting shorter every day. My ailments are increasing. I go to the barn once in a while and get out the cauldron. I put in the pot all kinds of things with frogs to ward off the hexes from my neighboring witch. I hang special necklaces around my neck. I sprinkle dust under my bed. But despite all my efforts, the curses continue and my life gets more difficult."

George told his story so well that I was almost convinced that there could be some truth in it.

One thing I remembered thinking, as he told the story, was that at the time of the witch trials, nobody was safe in Salem,

Massachusetts. Everyone there must have wondered who was responsible for all their troubles. Almost no one got out alive from under an accusation.

But then, George gave me some last good news. He asked, "Would you like to know what saves me?" I said, "Certainly."

He told me that he would be saved from everything that held him captive. He said, "I go to church every Sunday. There is something wonderful in the liturgy of the service. Jesus Christ saves me through his cross and resurrection."

When the drama was thoroughly played out, and we came back to reality, I wondered if I dared to tell him that there was no such thing as witchcraft. Well, I didn't! I felt I couldn't! Two weeks later, George died of a heart attack. I officiated at the funeral. I am sure that the whole community wondered, "What in the world is that young preacher going to say about George?" Well, I had some very positive things to say. Jesus was certainly central in the life of George. And along with the heavy baggage he was carrying around, he believed in the love of God in Jesus Christ. Yes, George was truly saved from his demons by Jesus Christ!

Now this story helps me ask you a question. If Jesus was born into a society that believed in demon possession, how do you think Jesus would react to people who were held captive by the superstitions of his day? Remember that there was a minority opinion with the priests that demons and devils did not exist. But Jesus never cited it. Jesus simply went up to the person and spoke his/her language and said to the demon, "Come out!" Jesus' strength of God was powerful, and the person possessed believed that the demons would flee from a power stronger than Satan's.

These are some of my reasons for not believing in the devil or Satan. And so like the Sadducees I cannot take some foreign ideas, pump them up with imaginative power, and call them "gods." There is but one God!

CHAPTER NINE

SUFFERING IS A PART OF LIFE

In Chapter Five we viewed some passages by the author of Deuteronomy and others about how God is described. One descriptive phrase was "God is one." In Deuteronomy 32:39, there was also a description of God's actions as a monotheistic God. It sounds like it's coming from God's mouth:

> "I kill and I make alive
> I wound and I heal."

Those two phrases are frightening if you recognize a God that tells you he is sending suffering. It sounds like God's will! And how about vs. 41b:

> I will take vengeance on my adversaries,
> and I will repay those who hate me.
> I will make my arrows drunk with blood,
> and my sword shall devour flesh—with
> the blood of the slain and the captives. . . .

To almost all people it sounds as if the one God sends suffering. But this one God is also described in Deuteronomy 32:4 as:

> The rock, his work is perfect,
> and all his ways are just.
> A faithful God, without deceit,
> just and upright is he.

Now we have a huge dilemma. If God is just, then how can God dole out pain and suffering? Here are new insights that the Jews discovered. God does not pass out pain and suffering indiscriminately, only as just punishment! According to the next level of old theologies: "Sin of human beings does bring pain and suffering." Some observations:

> First: Humans hurt humans (sin).
> Second: God punishes sinners.

So the answer is that human beings sin against everything and everybody for the Jews of Jesus' day was to find that:

- The earthly reign of the messiah that lasts forever for the faithful.
- All suffering and satanic enemies will be destroyed.
- The Messianic age begins on earth.

The reward for the Christians will come when:

- The faithful will be ushered into a new resurrected existence with Jesus Christ at the end of time.
- The heavenly reign of God will go on forever.

One night at class time I asked, "What two things must you do in life?"

One person said, "Die."

Another person said, "Pay taxes."

Isn't it a shame that both the things we have to do in life are seen as negatives?

"OK," I said, "I'll even add one more: we must suffer."

Wow, these three actions are so negative. Can't we turn them around a little and get a positive "something?" So, let's try to do just that. Are there three positive things we all will do in life?

1. We are born. We get started without our own help. That's a good thing!
2. We start growing and maturing. Hopefully, we can begin to think rationally and realize that paying taxes can be a positive. Paying taxes leads to things that are to our advantage: police and fire protection, 911 assistance, Federal, state, and local services. Let's get positive!
3. Life is not all suffering. There is happiness in this life, somewhere and sometime. Life is not all bad.

Conclusion: Suffering is just a part of life. What if someone wants to object and say, "God is powerful, God is almighty, God is capable of doing anything. He could even stop every bit of suffering. He's God for goodness sake!"

"So, let God stop suffering everywhere!"

Now, if we go along with this request, we must proceed this way. If God must stop all possibilities for suffering, then human life must be stopped. There could be no births, for there is suffering in it. You could not allow a baby to learn to walk because she might fall down and hurt herself. Human life would not be allowed. God could stop all suffering, but that would also stop living beings. If one person dared have an ache or pain, we would accuse God that life is not fair and not just.

But God has decided that there is human life, and God has made it the way it is. Suffering is a part of life. Let us help everyone accept that. Yes, suffering and "ouch" are a part of life. This creation is not possible without it. It is part and parcel with it.

Remember in chapter three we talked about the God of love. We saw how God created the universe with rules and constants.

There are laws that govern nature. To go against them allows suffering, pain, and hurt. This part of creation, "suffering," is somehow connected to God's creating the possibility of gladness and some happiness.

Be assured, it was in pure love that God created all things! All things are connected.

God said, "Let us make humankind in our image..." (Gen 1:26). "So God created humankind..."(Gen 1:27a).

This was God's will! And God is sustaining his creation. God is still active in the universe.

But now, I also say that God allows suffering as a part of life. This is a deep mystery. For some reason, all the pieces I have shown you about creation are necessary. The science, the physics, the mathematics, the quantum physics, and the chemistry all play a disciplined role in making life possible. In order to bring life to an actual beginning, all the disciplines must work together to work it into existence and sustain it. For some strange reason suffering is necessary to the life structure we have. Some people would say, "I'd just rather not have it, thank you!" But suffering seems to be there for some reason and helps to allow other things to be created, nurtured, and sustained from day to day.

Life by God's choice and decision has been created in such a way that human beings can exist. The rules of science make life possible; so, life exists. Remember the constant "gravity"? If it was any stronger than it is, life would not be possible. There are boundaries that make this world and universe possible. We must learn to accept them, or I would not be writing this right now.

Remember, God created the rules in and through his love. The rules give life the chance to continue for a long period of time. And life on earth was not supposed to be a "flash in the pan." There are patterns that are at work.

God is involved in the creation of constraints or boundaries of the law of nature. God stands behind the fine-tuned universe.

Gary E. Schwarz in his book *The G.O.D. Experiments*[1] points out how creation by chance is really unsupportable. Gary designed a simple experiment. He reports:

> I took some white sand, placed it on the bottom of a pot, and then made a simple sand painting with various colored grains of sand. One of the images sometimes painted by Native Americans is frogs. Frogs make me smile. I carefully dripped green and yellow grains of sand and created a mediocre cartoonlike Kermit the Frog sand painting. I originally used a round metal spaghetti pot with a cover—a square cardboard box with a cover works just as well. Even better is a clear plastic container so you can see the evolving process as it occurs. After my crude sand painting was completed, I covered the pot, and shook it once, opened it, and looked at what had happened to my cartoonlike Kermit. Then I re-covered the pot, shook it again, and took another look. I did this over and over, recording what I saw with each successive shaking. What do you think happened, over and over?
>
> To many people, experiments like my sand painting/shaking experiment might be viewed as a waste since any nincompoop knows in advance what the results will be. So why would a credentialed scientist bother? What I witnessed that day in the kitchen with my spaghetti pot was truly elementary, and it happened every time I shook the pan, the sand mixed and the frog was no longer.
>
> The more I shook the pan, the more the sand mixed. In the absence of constraints to maintain my original frog design, and in the absence of some sort of a Guiding, Organizing Designer taking a hand, the sand participated in a most remarkable and beautiful process. The process is simple and completely replicable.

---

1 Gary E. Schwartz, *The G.O.D. Experiments: How Science is Discovering God in Everything, Including Us*, Atria Books (now Simon and Schuster), 2006, pp. 31,32. Used by permission. All rights reserved.

The sand mixed. Blacks and whites, yellows and greens, whatever colors of sand were present, they were all brought together. They became a blended mixture, a family of colors, so to speak. They became a complex yet fairly uniform mixture of different colors.

Being a "show me" scientist, I insisted on replicating this experiment many times. Sometimes I began by creating an image of a frog, sometimes I began by writing the word 'frog'. Sometimes I drew a picture of a heart, sometimes I began by writing the word 'heart'—it didn't matter. When I went through the successive shaking of the pot, the result was always a blended mixture. Always. The sand always mixed, period. The conclusion is inexorable and unstoppable. In the absence of some part of Guiding-Organizing-Designing process, sand mixes. It mixes every single time.

In my university lectures, I have asked my undergraduate students at Harvard, Yale, and the University of Arizona if they have ever chanced upon a sand painting, either on beaches or in the desert. Once again, not one ever reported having seen spontaneous sand paintings.

If 'randomness' could indeed create sand paintings on beaches or on deserts—as the completely-chance-universe hypothesis predicts—how come no one has ever reported seeing a spontaneously created sand painting? Where are the sand paintings?

If chance cannot create simple sand paintings, then how can chance create an entire universe that is organized and evolving?

God is our creator!
There is another illustration that I have discovered that really helps understand that God created the presence of suffering.
Created Life, its structure, makeup, and sustenance has a created pattern of opposites.
Life is like a whole realm of coins.

Suffering Is a Part of Life

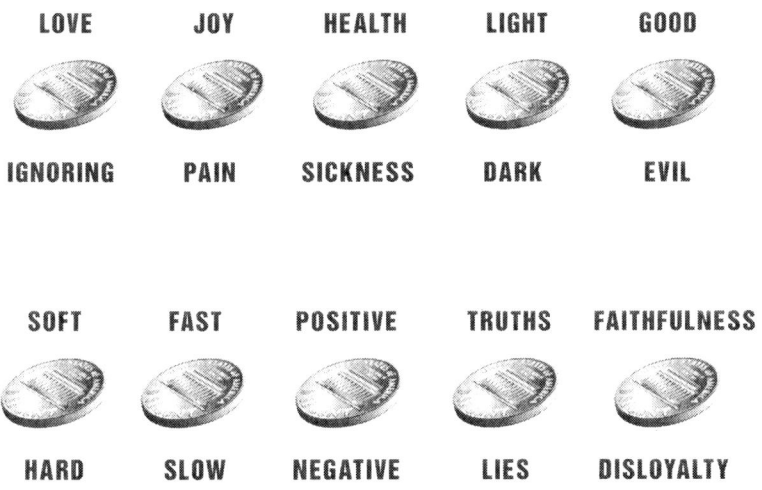

I cannot think of anything that does not have at least one counterbalancing phenomenon. There may be counter-balancing forces—powers that have many facets of counter balancing. But opposites are a part of creation. There are many coins that allow some real negative stuff.

HEALTHY BODIES

SICKNESS AND SUFFERING

This is just one.

There are many coins of opposites in nature. Some allow some pretty horrible stuff, but the pattern is fixed . . . opposites are in all things. In order to have one thing or one attribute—like sweetness—there is always the presence of the opposite—like sourness. So goes creation and life.

Creation was started with many building blocks. They are many-sided realities.

The instant that God decided there would be choices or options in this world, there would be coins of many sizes, many-faceted and dynamic. Suffering was a choice or option connected to an opposite. Enjoyment might be one of the choices on the other side of the coin from suffering.

Yes, suffering is a part of life by a choice and decision of our maker. Somewhere we need to begin to accept this reality. Suffering is not going away any time soon. Maybe this page about coins will give you something unique to think about and observe. It certainly has helped me stop protesting about all the bad stuff in life and blaming God for it. Nonsense.

Someone may ask, "So what's so good about suffering being a part of life?"

The instant that God decided there would be freedom in the new creation, the result was dynamic life in people and animals. We are free to be.

The coins are building blocks for freedom. I can still hear those voices: "God should have taken all suffering out of creation. So that no one could ever be hurt again. God is supreme, he could have done it!"

But for the greater Good, God left the opposites in, so that we would not have to be marionettes on strings in God's fingers. If we were marionettes, God could keep us from suffering, but there would be no freedom. He'd pull the string and I'd move. I wouldn't be allowed to do anything on my own. Why, I could hurt myself *and* blame God! If life had no choices or freedom, I could not even open my mouth to love God. God would have to pull the correct string, and my mouth would open and I'd automatically say, "I love You! I love You!"

Ladies and Gentlemen, I don't call that Love. God would never know if I really loved him unless I was free to work the other side of the coin, which would be to ignore God completely.

So freedom is a part of life. It can be a blessing or a curse. We can use the coin of freedom to help/hurt, give/take, act/sit still, appreciate/denigrate.

Why do we have synonyms and antonyms listed in dictionaries? They identify the coins of life. We are free to go in all directions. Of course, God would love His creation to reflect Him. This structure of life is a love gift from God. That way, when I say, "I love You God," God can believe me.

So in life, suffering is in there to allow an even greater life than if it was absent. God knows it's in there, but we have to accept some things in order to appreciate others.

Now saying all of this, is God going to be active in the world, break the rules, yank pain and suffering away out of its created placement? No. Can God work through suffering? Yes.

SUMMARY OF CHAPTER NINE
SUFFERING IS A PART OF LIFE

This chapter reviews all the points about suffering. Now add to these one coin that is especially important: Healthy Bodies (one side), Sickness and Suffering (another side). Suffering is a part of life, not some wild, unruly, evil presence.

A DIRECTION FOR THINKING:

How do the coins of creation help us see that suffering is a part of life in our ordered universe?

CHAPTER TEN

GOD CAN WORK THROUGH SUFFERING

Suffering is part of life.

The coin illustration is superb, for it shows that we have freedom to choose in all things at all times. We can act responsibly or we can have no care for anyone in the whole world but ourselves. The consequences and results from each will be those that come uniquely from the side we choose. We are free to bless or curse.

But there is another illustration which is superb in explaining another facet of how suffering becomes a part of life:

When a company makes steel, it follows a particular recipe. A metallurgist watches over and adjusts the process to achieve the stipulated different tolerances of each order. So workers prepare the raw material, add scrap iron with burnt lime and carbon, and put it into the large electric furnace. They add heat by electric power and by blowing oxygen into the furnace. The intense heat melts all the materials. The mixture melts and mixes together without going into solution. The burnt lime or CaO, when molten, pulls the impurities from the steel mixture. The CaO and the impurities have a lighter density, so they float to the top of the steel. The impurities must be drawn off before the steel is poured.

Every time steel is made, the process of chemical changes draws out the impurities, and it becomes a very hot liquid called slag. The slag is poured off, and then the clean steel is poured. You cannot have steel without slag forming as a by-product. Everybody wants steel. But in the process, slag is produced as well. Slag is the unwanted part of steel making. It is an unwanted reality. It just happens! It is a chemical by-product everyone could do without, but there it is. If you want steel, slag will be present.

Suffering is much like slag. Everyone wants happiness. But in a creation that allows choice and freedom, out pops the other side of happiness—suffering. Everyone will suffer sometime. Nobody wants it, but it happens. We would just as soon take it and dump it, but we cannot do that. At times, we go through suffering. We engage it, and God helps us through it. Wishing it away doesn't make it disappear. We have a God who can get involved with us to help us through the suffering.

Can God do anything with the slag of suffering? Or is God just letting suffering rage full blast through the ages and years? Yes, God can and does do something with the slag of suffering.

A. GOD CAN LEAD US TO HIMSELF.

I had a very painful surgery at age fifteen. God helped me through it. It was terrible to endure, but God brought me through it. For about five days, I was in a wheelchair. With another teenager on the surgery floor, we delivered mail and packages and ran errands. We talked to patients about their hurts and sufferings. I discovered the satisfaction of helping people. I actually remember the moments when I reflected on that in the hospital. And God was there as I healed.

Once, as a pastor, I was in a home visiting a prospective member. There was much noise, shouting, and laughing as a group of men came bounding in the house with beers in their hands. They looked sweaty and bedraggled. When they came into our room, the lady of the house said, "This is the pastor of the church I'm attending!"

The group of men altered their speech, lowered the volume, and became a little sheepish. They tried to hide their beers and their smokes. They then started to laugh and snicker at the situation and seemed to imply, "What in the world is he doing here?" Some people have no desire to have anything to do with God.

But when suffering comes to them, they will ask, "Why me?" and then, maybe, they might ask the question, "Why me, *God*?" And then they might say, "God, come to me! Help me!" With the slag of suffering, God can get in there, if wanted, and fill a heart and soul with love and healing. It just is so. But the help through suffering is always after the fact. God did not bring the suffering, but after the suffering starts we can invite God in, maybe for the first time, to help us through it.

Why would God want to do this? Because God loves us! God wants a relationship with us! He wants to show us the cross of Jesus and the resurrection. God wants to save everyone in the whole wide world from sin and death.

Yet some people do not want to be led to God.

B. GOD WANTS TO REDUCE SUFFERING.

Despite this assurance of God's love for us, many people fight back when they suffer and say, "It's all God's fault!" As a matter of fact, the opposite is true. God is not satisfied to allow suffering to run rampant. Every day of human history, God has been involved in getting rid of suffering. This is God's will of love.

God does work in and through people and things to reduce the amount of suffering.

Who were the first scientists and doctors who cared for people? Christians.

Who were some of the first people to have hospitals, clinics, and concerns for people in pain? Christians.

Today, through medical science, the march to reduce suffering is on worldwide. Treatments and drugs are evolving into better procedures and medicines that take away suffering and provide for more happiness.

Let me illustrate God's will to reduce suffering.

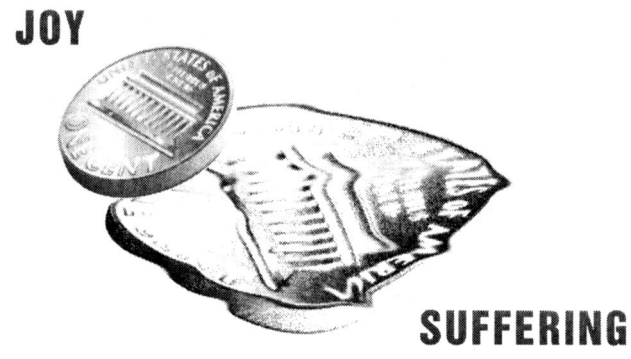

With the massive research and instrumentation of medical science around the world, suffering is being reduced. People are living longer. Advances in science in the health field are multiplying. God is helping with new discoveries that lessen suffering—discoveries such as anesthesia.

I asked my doctor, "Name some diseases that are not a threat at this time." He wrote small pox, chicken pox, rubella. I might put down polio. But there are a few cases here and there. It is such a joy to reduce suffering by eradicating some diseases. Thank you God! And God works his will even through non-Christian physicians. How? They give good doctoring even if they are atheists and do it for the money. God's will is being done, and they often do not know it. Neither did Pontius Pilate know that his actions would manifest the will of God.

Another important ongoing discovery lies in the field of genetics. This will end up being a huge gift from God for generations to come. Genetic identification allows for behavior and alternative actions that can lessen or avoid future suffering. As time goes on, we will be able to change, alter, or eliminate some diseases and lessen the symptoms of others. There is great potential through discovery and research in genetics.

In this small book, we have investigated the Jewish search for an answer to suffering. First, we realized there were two early traditions. One answer meshed with the belief in a monotheistic God. The results could have accused God of sending suffering. We rejected this answer.

We then began to see another answer emerge through the firm belief that God is *just*. We saw that human beings bring suffering into the world. And that is sin. A just God will punish sin, period. We abbreviated this theology as follows:

> Do good; receive goodness. Do bad; receive evil.

We saw that although human beings are responsible for their own suffering most of the time, there are times when sufferers are completely innocent, so we rejected this long-held formula. But it is still in the hearts and minds of many people today. Looking for a way to fill the hole of innocent suffering, we saw how the notions of Satan and dualism emerged when the people of Israel were in exile in Babylon.

After the people of Israel returned from the exile, they brought this baggage with them. The devil/satan and his cohorts of demons were ruining people's lives with havoc and suffering. These fiends attacked everyone, sinner or righteous. Not all Jews believed in this answer!

I hope when you think about suffering and its origin you will have graduated from saying it is God's pleasure or displeasure to give you suffering. I hope you pick something else as the origin of suffering like human beings, or Satan, or suffering as a part of life. One will help you when suffering comes your way. The others will not.

Grief is one of the worst emptying devastations that can grip a person. Loss of a family member or friend can cause intense grief and suffering. Pastor John Claypool in his book *Tracks of a Fellow Struggler:*

Living and Growing Through Grief[1], chronicles his struggle with the loss of his eight-year-old daughter. Even in the darkness of the pain and suffering, John Claypool said gratitude was one way out of the deep darkness: "The way of gratitude does not alleviate pain, but it somehow puts some light around the darkness and builds strength to begin to move on."

The following passage by Pastor Claypool is a powerful story. You will understand it better if you see suffering as a part of life.

> A little something that happened to me years ago may help you to understand what I mean. When World War II started, my family did not have a washing machine. With gas rationed and the laundry several miles away, keeping our clothes clean became an intensely practical problem. One of my father's younger business associates was drafted and his wife prepared to go with him, and we offered to let them store their furniture in our basement. Quite unexpectedly, they suggested that we use their washing machine while they were gone. "It would be better for it to be running," they said, "than sitting up rusting." So this is what we did, and it helped us a great deal.
>
> Since I used to help with the washing, across the years I developed quite an affectionate relationship for that old green Bendix. But eventually the war ended, and our friends returned, and in the meantime I had forgotten how the machine had come to be in our basement in the first place. When they came and took it, I was terribly upset and I said so quite openly.
>
> But my mother, being the wise woman she is, sat me down and put things in perspective for me. She said, "Wait a minute son. You must remember that machine never belonged to us in the first place. That we ever got to use it at all was a gift. So, instead of being mad at its being taken away let's use this occasion to be grateful that we had it at all."

---

[1] Morehead Publishing, 2004, pp. 63, 64. Used by permission. All rights reserved.

Gratitude makes life bearable. Suffering is bound to come to all of us. How you view it will have a bearing on your mind, heart, and spirit. God desires to help you through it.

SUMMARY OF CHAPTER TEN
GOD CAN WORK THROUGH SUFFERING

God can and does work through suffering. This chapter explores how God works in this way.

> A. Suffering is a part of life. It is but one side of a coin of opposites.
>
> B. Suffering is present much like slag is a part of the steel-making process. Slag is unwanted, but it shows up anyway. It is a product of the chemical reaction that creates steel.
>
> C. God is also present, ever reducing suffering for everyone and everything.

Suffering always appears in a creation with freedom. We should give thanks to God for the good times. Gratitude for the good is the best way to deal with life. That, too, is a part of life.

A DIRECTION FOR THINKING

If suffering is a part of life, how does God get involved in relieving suffering and help us through that suffering?

CHAPTER ELEVEN

CLOSING THOUGHTS

Here are some more thoughts to help us be appreciative despite suffering.

God does not send suffering, but God will be present through it and perhaps lead us to a good purpose. I mentioned in the previous chapter that when I was fifteen, I had a terrible surgery. I had a 50 percent chance that it would be successful. It was more painful than I ever thought it would be. My parents told me long after the surgery was completed that when they returned to my room immediately after the surgery, I was as white as the sheets on my bed! That was one hellish night of suffering and agony.

Yet at no time did I ever think or believe or say to God, "You brought this." What I learned from the experience was that God used it for good purposes. He used it after the fact of suffering. I will never blame it on God. God never wanted me to suffer. But other things got in the middle and created a problem with my body. The surgeon said, "You're going in there, Landis, and let's get it done." I had the surgery!

God did not send this suffering to me. But God did use it later to arouse my interest in becoming a pastor. The surgery and its aftermath were tough experiences, but the longer-term outcome was rewarding. I hope you will not have to suffer like I did. But many of you will suffer, and some of you may suffer even more than I did. If it happens to you, please remember, it is not God's will. God is not doing that to you. There are other factors that have done it. But God can use that event and suffering for your good and His purposes. Your life can and will be better for it. You can count on it. It is a promise. God promises to be with you wherever and whatever you suffer. God comes close to us, His people, and renews our spirits and our lives.

You may have paused at some of the words God spoke to Mack in the novel *The Shack* by William Paul Young[1]. I did! God says, "Mack, just because I work incredible good out of unspeakable tragedies doesn't mean I orchestrate the tragedies. Don't you ever assume that my using something means I caused it or that I needed it to accomplish my purposes." That's a neat way to express this truth.

There is one more outstanding story that I share with you because it may change your mind about saying, "It's God's will." It is from Leslie D. Weatherhead's book *The Will of God*[2]. In one of the sermons in this marvelous book, Leslie Weatherhead tells a true story:

> The matter came to me most poignantly when I was in India. I was standing on the veranda of an Indian home darkened by bereavement. My Indian friend had lost his little son, the light of his eyes, in a cholera epidemic. At the far end of the veranda his little daughter, the only remaining child, slept in a cot covered with a mosquito net. We paced up and down, and I tried in my clumsy way to comfort and console him. But he said, "Well, padre, it is the will of God. That's all there is to it. It is the will of God."

---

1 Windblown Media, 2007, p. 187.

2 Abingdon Press, 1944, p. 10. Used by permission. All rights reserved.

Fortunately, I knew him well enough to be able to reply without being misunderstood, and I said something like this: "Supposing someone crept up these steps onto the veranda tonight, while you all slept, and deliberately put a wad of cotton soaked in cholera germ culture over your little girl's mouth as she lay in that cot there on the veranda, what would you think about that?"

"My God," he said, "what would I think about that? Nobody would do such a damnable thing. If he attempted it and I caught him, I would kill him with as little compunction as I would a snake, and throw him over the veranda. What do you mean by suggesting such a thing?"

"But, John," I said quietly, "isn't that just what you have accused God of doing when you said it was his will? Call your little boy's death the result of mass ignorance, call it mass folly, call it mass sin, if you like, call it bad drains or communal carelessness, but don't call it the will of God. Surely we cannot identify as the will of God something for which a man would be locked up in jail, or put in a criminal lunatic asylum."

Leslie Weatherhead continues, "Those who want a text for this sermon will find it in the eighteenth chapter of St. Matthew's Gospel and the fourteenth verse: 'It is not the will of your Father which is in heaven, that one of these little ones should perish.'"

Let me broaden it even further. It is not the will of God to have any person perish! God is not a murderer; God is a savior. It is God's will to save us through Jesus. Jesus suffered terribly. In the Garden of Gethsemane, Jesus said, "Put the sword away. Shall I not drink the cup which the father has given me?" That's God's will, and Jesus accepted it.

Did you hear that? Jesus suffered to save us from sin and death. Yes, Jesus suffered, and He had done no wrong. He was sinless. Jesus did not have to suffer and die. He was perfect, and yet he willingly suffered for us. Jesus did not deserve his suffering and death. But he would do all for us. That is servanthood!

What about Christians? Are they exempt from suffering? If you ever hear a Christian say, "Because I'm a follower of Jesus, or if I do everything right, I should not have to suffer," you just tell them to take a look at Jesus. Or tell them to look at Charlotte. At one of my congregations, some years ago, I was teaching some of this material in a "life with God" course. Bill's wife Charlotte was in the hospital with three different diseases. She was suffering more than any person I have ever known in my forty-four years of ministry.

Bill was understandably most attentive in the class. When it was over, we exchanged the latest news about Charlotte. We chatted some more about the material, and Bill went home. I could tell it was helping him let loose of his former ways of thinking about suffering. Charlotte died soon after this particular class. The first family visitation was on a Friday night. I could imagine the pathos of the crowd at the funeral home with a father and two young children.

On Saturday morning, I was in the narthex of the church when Bill drove up in his car. He got out of his car and came to the door. I could tell by the look on his face that he was a very determined man. Bill stormed into the narthex and came over to me with a face about to explode.

"I almost hit a woman last night at the visitation!" He told me that an acquaintance of the family came through the receiving line and that when she got to Bill, she said with some conviction, "Bill, it was God's will." Bill told me that he was very close to popping her. He went on, "I told her that it wasn't God's will. God did not kill my wife: the disease did! And it was God's will that Jesus Christ saved her from sin and death, and she's alive with Jesus right now!" We talked more about the incident. He thanked me for the classes. We prayed, and Bill left. Wow, what a witness! Death is a part of life, and it is God's will to help us all the way to eternal life.

As I did with Bill, through this book I have been trying to get the reader to refrain from saying, "Suffering is from God" or "It's God's will."

So where does suffering come from?

Call it: *Sin*

Call it: *the nature of human beings*
Call it: *Satan*
Call it: *A part of life*
But don't call it the will of God!

God does not bring suffering, but after the fact, God surely desires to use it for His own purposes and yours as well.

I want to end with a very haunting story. The people in this story are a father and his son. It is a cute vignette. But then God quietly enters the story, and He tells us a Holy Comfort, (I will be with you always).

A father in Michigan tells how his son learned to play hide-and-seek with him in a small wood beside their home. The lad would hide behind a tree, eagerly enjoying the father's loud complaint: "Where's Christopher? I can't find Christopher!" Then the child would burst out, "Here, Daddy. Look for me here behind this tree."

In the human game, God is often hidden from us—off in the woods behind some tree. We seek God in the pleasant and open places of life . . . in the garden, not in the woods. But it is in the dark forest of our suffering that God's voice cries out: *"Here, look for me here!"*

May God's peace be with you, even in your suffering.

SUMMARY OF CHAPTER ELEVEN
CLOSING THOUGHTS

Here are some stories that help us accept life the way it is and give thanks for it. The coins of life are the created order for possibilities and freedom. There are choices and we make them every day. Our choices can work to eliminate the suffering that is a part of life.

We are allowed to blame suffering on many things. But I hope that you have moved from blaming toward a more practical understanding of life, one that does not blame God for suffering but seeks God even in suffering

A DIRECTION FOR THINKING:

How does this chapter give you some solace and peace? How has it given you a new way to think about suffering?

epilogue

In order to get some feelings, insights, and reasonings about suffering, we begin at the top! Out of God's character the creation bursts, beautiful to behold. Out of God's nature we can see how the three constants call forth a loving creation. Saying this, the freedom must always allow choices. And there is a spectrum of choices through creation. God leavens life and allows it to *breathe*. Life ebbs and flows. That is the way it is supposed to be.

Sometimes within the ebbs and flows of life suffering shows up. It is a part of life. There are consequences for all actions. Some are not pleasant. Actions and consequences are tied together in creation.

From this, I can better grasp the whole scope of what we call suffering. From heaven, reasoning downward, we can understand the words *acceptance* of life. God created the universe this way. Hopefully, we can see this love.

Within these pages, we decided very early on that to understand the environment of suffering we had to step back from the tragedies and pains. We looked to God to speak to us about his creation and plans. Like Baby, my kitty cat, we sit and look and listen to the sounds of the creation around us. At times, we too do not understand or perceive or feel the purpose of life.

Because of her *catness*, Baby accepts things the way they are. Within her she is always hoping for love, kindness, caring, and safety. She needs to eat and drink. When she feels these things present in her life, she purrs.

Baby accepts the possibilities of some negatives in *catness*, and she tries to be very careful to avoid pain, hurt, danger, and insecurity. Loud sounds and fast movements frighten her. They could mean predators are attacking from somewhere near. But when there is peace and security, she purrs. "Thank you," she says to the human angels she adopted. Love passes between animal and human being.

So in the midst of all of life, settle in with the Holy One and dare to enjoy. Yes, always be careful, for there is another side with scary dangers. The coins of existence are always around. Trust life enough to dare to enjoy. Go ahead— connect with your creator and Lord—Purr!

acknowledgments

I fondly remember all my students in the extended courses of "Life with God" and "Crossways" beginning in the 1980s. Some of my students heard portions of this book and came to me stating, "Write this down. We never heard suffering explained so clearly."

I became a supervisor of candidates for the ordained ministry in the Lutheran Church of America. Many of my interns would say, "Write this down."

One of my interns, Rev. David Ritchie of Ironton, Ohio, exhorted me every time we communicated. He'd say, "Landis, write it down!"

In 2009 I took my teaching notes and outlines and readied the material for a book. I jumped in with both feet writing the first draft. I want to thank my typist, Iva Johnson and Diane Chambers for reviewing the material for structure and language.

I want to thank Annmarie Demko for helping me with all kinds of communications during this process.

I want to thank Karen Kaufman, Director of the Resource Center of the Northeastern Ohio Synod of The Evangelical Lutheran Church of America. She gave me options about connections needed in the publication process. She gave many literary suggestions that now appear in the book.

I thank Pat Hardwick, a Scrabble tournament player, for suggesting the title of this book "The Price of Being Alive."

I also want to thank Bill Huff and Huff Publishing Associates for their expertise and foresight in the publication process.

And then to God who I sensed was urging me to "Write it down!" Thank you.

Landis Coffman
July 27, 2011

biography

The Reverend R. Landis Coffman, Jr., is a native of Hagerstown, Maryland. He graduated from Bucknell University with a Bachelor's Degree in Business Administration and from the Lutheran Theological Seminary, Gettysburg, Pennsylvania, with a Masters of Divinity Degree. He interned with the Pittsburgh Lutheran Service Society and received his clinical training at West Penn Hospital. He has taken study tours of Israel, Turkey, Greece and Egypt.

He has served as Pastor at St. Matthews Lutheran Church, Plainfield, Pennsylvania; Peace Lutheran Church, Connersville, Indiana; Saint John Lutheran Church, East Liverpool, Ohio; Prince of Peace Lutheran Church, Westlake, Ohio; Messiah Lutheran Church, Reynoldsburg, Ohio. At present, he is serving as pastor at Holy Trinity Lutheran Church in Akron, Ohio.

Pastor Coffman has become known for his inspiring sermons, children's messages and his teaching of Biblical courses such as "Life with God" and "Crossways." Insight and knowledge gained from biblical study tours to the Middle East enriched his ministry. Pastor Coffman's use of his hobby of ventriloquism enables him to give some special children's sermons. He is often called upon as a motivational speaker at civic and school functions. Pastor Coffman, on behalf of the seminary, has been a teacher for the process called Supervision, in which new supervisors learn in order to give the greatest amount of learning in the intern year.

Judy Coffman is a native of Berlin, Pennsylvania. She is a retired registered nurse and received her training at West Penn Hospital in Pittsburgh. She presently works in a physician's office with patients.

The Coffmans have two children, Christina and Craig. Christina is a certified gemologist and working in the San Diego, California area. Craig is a CFO for a business near the University of Cincinnati, Ohio.